THE PASSION

OF OUR LORD

ACCORDING TO

LUKE

FOR CONGREGATIONAL READING

THE PASSION OF OUR LORD ACCORDING TO

LUKE

SPEAKING PARTS:

NARRATOR	SERVANT
JESUS	WITNESS
PETER	PILATE
PEOPLE	FIRST CRIMINAL
CENTURION	SECOND CRIMINAL

The congregation will read in unison the part of the People, which is in bold type and marked by the symbol ✠.

SERIES C

Luke 22:1—23:56

(New Revised Standard Version)

NARRATOR: The Passion of our Lord Jesus Christ according to Saint Luke.

Now the festival of Unleavened Bread, which is called the Passover, was near. The chief priests and the scribes were looking for a way to put Jesus to death, for they were afraid of the people.

Then Satan entered into Judas called Iscariot, who was one of the twelve; he went away and conferred with the chief priests and officers of the temple police about how he might betray Jesus to them. They were greatly pleased and agreed to give him money. So he consented and began to look for an opportunity to betray him to them when no crowd was present.

Then came the day of Unleavened Bread, on which the Passover lamb had to be sacrificed. So Jesus sent Peter and John, saying,

JESUS: Go and prepare the Passover meal for us that we may eat it.

NARRATOR: They asked him,

PETER: Where do you want us to make preparations for it?

JESUS: Listen, when you have entered the city, a man carrying a jar of water will meet you; follow him into the house he enters and say to the owner of the house, "The teacher asks you, 'Where is the guest room, where I may eat the Passover with my disciples?'" He will show you a large room upstairs, already furnished. Make preparations for us there.

NARRATOR: So they went and found everything as he had told them; and they prepared the Passover meal.

When the hour came, he took his place at the table, and the apostles with him. He said to them,

JESUS: I have eagerly desired to eat this Passover with you before I suffer; for I tell you, I will not eat it until it is fulfilled in the kingdom of God.

NARRATOR: Then he took a cup, and after giving thanks he said,

JESUS: Take this and divide it among yourselves; for I tell you that from now on I will not drink of the fruit of the vine until the kingdom of God comes.

NARRATOR: Then he took a loaf of bread, and when he had given thanks, he broke it and gave it to them, saying,

JESUS: This is my body, which is given for you. Do this in remembrance of me.

NARRATOR: And he did the same with the cup after supper, saying,

JESUS: This cup that is poured out for you is the new covenant in my blood. But see, the one who betrays me is with me, and his hand is on the table. For the Son of Man is going as it has been determined, but woe to that one by whom he is betrayed!

NARRATOR: Then they began to ask one another, which one of them it could be who would do this.

A dispute also arose among them as to which one of them was to be regarded as the greatest. But he said to them,

JESUS: The kings of the Gentiles lord it over them; and those in authority over them are called benefactors. But not so with you; rather the greatest among you must become like the youngest, and the leader like one who serves. For who is greater, the one who is at the table or the one who serves? Is it not the one at the table? But I am among you as one who serves.

You are those who have stood by me in my trials; and I confer on you, just as my Father has conferred on me, a kingdom, so that you may eat and drink at my table in my kingdom, and you will sit on thrones judging the twelve tribes of Israel.

Simon, Simon, listen! Satan has demanded to sift all of you like wheat, but I have prayed for you that your own faith may not fail; and you, when once you have turned back, strengthen your brothers.

NARRATOR: And Peter said to him,

PETER: Lord, I am ready to go with you to prison and to death!

NARRATOR: Jesus said,

JESUS: I tell you, Peter, the cock will not crow this day, until you have denied three times that you know me.

NARRATOR: He said to them,

JESUS: When I sent you out without a purse, bag, or sandals, did you lack anything?

NARRATOR: They said,

✠ **No, not a thing.**

NARRATOR: He said to them,

JESUS: But now, the one who has a purse must take it, and likewise a bag. And the one who has no sword must sell his cloak and buy one. For I tell you, this scripture must be fulfilled in me, "And he was counted among the lawless"; and indeed what is written about me is being fulfilled.

NARRATOR: They said,

✠ **Lord, look, here are two swords.**

NARRATOR: He replied,

JESUS: It is enough.

NARRATOR: He came out and went, as was his custom, to the Mount of Olives; and the disciples followed him. When he reached the place, he said to them,

JESUS: Pray that you may not come into the time of trial.

NARRATOR: Then he withdrew from them about a stone's throw, knelt down, and prayed,

JESUS: Father, if you are willing, remove this cup from me; yet, not my will but yours be done.

NARRATOR: Then an angel from heaven appeared to him and gave him strength. In his anguish he prayed more earnestly, and his sweat became like great drops of blood falling down on the ground. When he got up from prayer, he came to the disciples and found them sleeping because of grief, and he said to them,

JESUS: Why are you sleeping? Get up and pray that you may not come into the time of trial.

NARRATOR: While he was still speaking, suddenly a crowd came, and the one called Judas, one of the twelve, was leading them. He approached Jesus to kiss him; but Jesus said to him,

JESUS: Judas, is it with a kiss that you are betraying the Son of Man?

NARRATOR: When those who were around him saw what was coming, they asked,

✠ **Lord, should we strike with the sword?**

NARRATOR: Then one of them struck the slave of the high priest and cut off his right ear. But Jesus said,

JESUS: No more of this!

NARRATOR: And he touched his ear and healed him. Then Jesus said to the chief priests, the officers of the temple police, and the elders who had come for him,

JESUS: Have you come out with swords and clubs as if I were a bandit? When I was with you day after day in the temple, you did not lay hands on me. But this is your hour, and the power of darkness!

NARRATOR: Then they seized him and led him away, bringing him into the high priest's house. But Peter was following at a distance. When they had kindled a fire in the middle of the courtyard and sat down together, Peter sat among them. Then a servant-girl, seeing him in the firelight, stared at him and said,

SERVANT: This man also was with him.

NARRATOR: But he denied it, saying,

PETER: Woman, I do not know him.

NARRATOR: A little later someone else, on seeing him, said,

WITNESS: You also are one of them.

NARRATOR: But Peter said,

PETER: Man, I am not!

NARRATOR: Then about an hour later still another kept insisting,

WITNESS: Surely this man also was with him; for he is a Galilean.

NARRATOR: But Peter said,

PETER: Man, I do not know what you are talking about!

NARRATOR: At that moment, while he was still speaking, the cock crowed. The Lord turned and looked at Peter. Then Peter remembered the word of the Lord, how he had said to him, "Before the cock crows today, you will deny me three times." And he went out and wept bitterly.

Now the men who were holding Jesus began to mock him and beat him; they also blindfolded him and kept asking him,

✠ **Prophesy! Who is it that struck you?**

NARRATOR: They kept heaping many other insults on him.

When day came, the assembly of the elders of the people, both chief priests and scribes, gathered together, and they brought him to their council. They said,

✠ **If you are the Messiah, tell us.**

NARRATOR: He replied,

JESUS: If I tell you, you will not believe; and if I question you, you will not answer. But from now on the Son of Man will be seated at the right hand of the power of God.

NARRATOR: All of them asked,

✠ **Are you, then, the Son of God?**

NARRATOR: He said to them,

JESUS: You say that I am.

NARRATOR: Then they said,

✠ **What further testimony do we need? We have heard it ourselves from his own lips!**

NARRATOR: Then the assembly rose as a body and brought Jesus before Pilate. They began to accuse him, saying,

✠ **We found this man perverting our nation, forbidding us to pay taxes to the emperor, and saying that he himself is the Messiah, a king.**

NARRATOR: Then Pilate asked him,

PILATE: Are you the king of the Jews?

NARRATOR: He answered,

JESUS: You say so.

NARRATOR: Then Pilate said to the chief priests and the crowds,

PILATE: I find no basis for an accusation against this man.

NARRATOR: But they were insistent and said,

✠ **He stirs up the people by teaching throughout all Judea, from Galilee where he began even to this place.**

NARRATOR: When Pilate heard this, he asked whether the man was a Galilean. And when he learned that he was under Herod's jurisdiction, he sent him off to Herod, who was himself in Jerusalem at that time.

When Herod saw Jesus, he was very glad, for he had been wanting to see him for a long time, because he had heard about him and was hoping to see him perform some sign. He questioned him at some length, but Jesus gave him no answer. The chief priests and the scribes stood by, vehemently accusing him. Even Herod with his soldiers treated him with contempt and mocked him; then he put an elegant robe on him, and sent him back to Pilate. That same day Herod and Pilate became friends with each other; before this they had been enemies.

Pilate then called together the chief priests, the leaders, and the people, and said to them,

PILATE: You brought me this man as one who was perverting the people; and here I have examined him in your presence and have not found this man guilty of any of your charges against him. Neither has Herod, for he sent him back to us. Indeed, he has done nothing to deserve death. I will therefore have him flogged and release him.

NARRATOR: Then they all shouted out together,

✠ **Away with this fellow! Release Barabbas for us!**

NARRATOR: (This was a man who had been put in prison for an insurrection that had taken place in the city, and for murder.) Pilate, wanting to release Jesus, addressed them again; but they kept shouting,

✠ **Crucify, crucify him!**

NARRATOR: A third time Pilate said to them,

PILATE: Why, what evil has he done? I have found in him no ground for the sentence of death; I will therefore have him flogged and then release him.

NARRATOR: But they kept urgently demanding with loud shouts that he should be crucified; and their voices prevailed. So Pilate gave his verdict that their demand should be granted. He released the man they asked for, the one who had been put in prison for insurrection and murder, and he handed Jesus over as they wished.

As they led him away, they seized a man, Simon of Cyrene, who was coming from the country, and they laid the cross on him, and made him carry it behind Jesus. A great number of the people followed him, and among them were women who were beating their breasts and wailing for him. But Jesus turned to them and said,

JESUS: Daughters of Jerusalem, do not weep for me, but weep for yourselves and for your children. For the days are surely coming when they will say, "Blessed are the barren, and the wombs that never bore, and the breasts that never nursed." Then they will begin to say to the mountains, "Fall on us"; and to the hills, "Cover us." For if they do this when the wood is green, what will happen when it is dry?

NARRATOR: Two others also, who were criminals, were led away to be put to death with him. When they came to the place that is called The Skull, they crucified Jesus there with the criminals, one on his right and one on his left. Then Jesus said,

JESUS: Father, forgive them; for they do not know what they are doing.

NARRATOR: And they cast lots to divide his clothing. And the people stood by, watching; but the leaders scoffed at him, saying,

✠ **He saved others; let him save himself if he is the Messiah of God, his chosen one!**

NARRATOR: The soldiers also mocked him, coming up and offering him sour wine, and saying,

WITNESS: If you are the King of the Jews, save yourself!

NARRATOR: There was also an inscription over him, "This is the King of the Jews."

One of the criminals who were hanged there kept deriding him and saying,

FIRST CRIMINAL: Are you not the Messiah? Save yourself and us!

NARRATOR: But the other rebuked him, saying,

SECOND CRIMINAL: Do you not fear God, since you are under the same sentence of condemnation? And we indeed have been condemned justly, for we are getting what we deserve for our deeds, but this man has done nothing wrong.

NARRATOR: Then he said,

SECOND CRIMINAL: Jesus, remember me when you come into your kingdom.

NARRATOR: Jesus replied,

JESUS: Truly I tell you, today you will be with me in Paradise.

NARRATOR: It was now about noon, and darkness came over the whole land until three in the afternoon, while the sun's light failed; and the curtain of the temple was torn in two. Then Jesus, crying with a loud voice, said,

JESUS: Father, into your hands I commend my spirit.

NARRATOR: Having said this, he breathed his last.

(*Silence*)

When the centurion saw what had taken place, he praised God and said,

CENTURION: Certainly this man was innocent.

NARRATOR: And when all the crowds who had gathered there for this spectacle saw what had taken place, they returned home, beating their breasts. But all his acquaintances, including the women who had followed him from Galilee, stood at a distance, watching these things.

Now there was a good and righteous man named Joseph, who, though a member of the council, had not agreed to their plan and action. He came from the Jewish town of Arimathea, and he was waiting expectantly for the kingdom of God. This man went to Pilate and asked for the body of Jesus. Then he took it down, wrapped it in a linen cloth, and laid it in a rock-hewn tomb where no one had ever been laid. It was the day of Preparation, and the sabbath was beginning. The women who had come with him from Galilee followed, and they saw the tomb and how his body was laid. Then they returned, and prepared spices and ointments.

On the sabbath they rested according to the commandment.

Design: Koechel Peterson and Associates, Inc.

Printed in the U.S.A.

4 5 6 7 8 9 0 1 2 3 4 5 6 7 8 9

Augsburg Fortress

ISBN 0-8066-0569-3

3-5165